NATIONAL GEOGRAPHIC

T0303045

CIVILIZATIONS PAST TO PRESENT

THE VIKING WORLD

ANN M. ROSSI

PICTURE CREDITS
Cover Premium Stock/Corbis; page 3 (top) Bo Zaunders/Corbis; pages 3 (bottom), 10 (right), 20 (bottom) C. M. Dixon; pages 4–5 Hubert Stadler/Corbis; pages 7 (top), 21 (top) Taxi/Getty Images; page 7 (bottom) Archivo Iconografico, S.A./Corbis, page 8 Louis S. Glanzman/National Geographic Image Collection; page 9 Michael Freeman/Corbis; page 10 (left) Ludovic Maisant/Corbis; page 11 Hans Madej/Bilderberg/Aurora Photos; page 12 Wolfgang Kaehler/Corbis; page 13 Charles and Josette Lenars/Corbis; pages 14, 20 (top) Stone/Getty Images; page 15 Ted Spiegel/Corbis; page 16 Scala/Art Resource, NY; page 17 (left) Layne Kennedy/Corbis; page 17 (right) James Davis, Eye Ubiquitous/Corbis; pages 18 (top), 23 Werner Forman/Corbis; page 18 (bottom) National Museum of Fine Arts, Stockholm; page 19 Brian A. Vikander/Corbis; page 21 (bottom) Macduff Everton/Corbis; page 22 The Image Bank/Getty Images; page 24 D.Y./Art Resource, NY.

Produced through the worldwide resources of the National Geographic Society, John M. Fahey, Jr., President and Chief Executive Officer; Gilbert M. Grosvenor, Chairman of the Board; Nina D. Hoffman, Executive Vice President and President, Books and Education Publishing Group.

PREPARED BY NATIONAL GEOGRAPHIC SCHOOL PUBLISHING
Ericka Markman, Senior Vice President and President, Children's Books and Education Publishing Group; Steve Mico, Vice President, Editorial Director; Marianne Hiland, Executive Editor; Anita Schwartz, Project Editor; Jim Hiscott, Design Manager; Kristin Hanneman, Illustrations Manager; Diana Bourdrez, Picture Editor; Matt Wascavage, Manager of Publishing Services; Sean Philpotts, Production Manager.

MANUFACTURING AND QUALITY CONTROL
Christopher A. Liedel, Chief Financial Officer; Phillip L. Schlosser, Director; Clifton M. Brown, Manager.

PROGRAM DEVELOPMENT
Gare Thompson Associates, Inc.

ART DIRECTION
Dan Banks, Project Design Company

BOOK DEVELOPMENT
Nieman Inc.

CONSULTANTS/REVIEWERS
Dr. Margit E. McGuire, School of Education, Seattle University, Seattle, Washington

BOOK DESIGN
Three Communication Design, LLC

PICTURE EDITING AND MANAGEMENT
Corrine L. Brock

MAP DEVELOPMENT AND PRODUCTION
Bruce Burdick

Published by the National Geographic Society
1145 17th Street, N.W.
Washington, D.C. 20036-4688

ISBN: 0-7922-4541-5
ISBN-13: 978-0-7922-4541-4

Fourth Printing July 2012
Printed in Canada

Cover: A fishing village on a small island between Iceland and Norway

page 3 (top): A fjord in Norway

page 3 (bottom): A pin used to hold a Viking dress

CONTENTS

Introduction 4
The Viking World: Then and Now 6
Community Life 8
Ships, Trade, and Exploration 14
Religion and Rune Stones 18
Entertainment 20
Contributions 22
Glossary 23
Index 24

INTRODUCTION

Imagine sailing in a fast, narrow ship whose prow, or front, is shaped like a dragon's head. Think of how it would feel to wear a shirt made of heavy iron rings. Could you move on skates made out of horse bones? Imagine living in a room heated only by a wood fire or bathing only once a week in a steam bath.

These are some of the things that you might have done had you lived during the Viking Age.

The **Vikings** lived more than 1,000 years ago. They came from the part of northern Europe that is now called **Scandinavia**.

Thingvellir, the place where Vikings held meetings in Iceland

They were so fierce that people were afraid of them. Traveling by sea, they raided towns, stealing and killing. They also traded with other peoples and settled new lands. In their long warships, the Vikings sailed to faraway places, such as Greenland, Russia, and even America!

We come into contact with the Vikings every Tuesday, Wednesday, Thursday, and Friday. Those days are named for Viking gods.

There is much to discover about the people of Scandinavia, past and present. So, let's begin our journey.

THE VIKING WORLD: THEN AND NOW

Viking Settlements, A.D. 700–1100

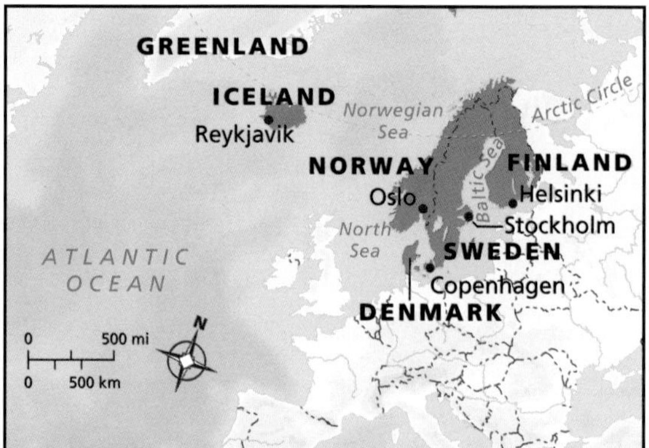

Scandinavia Today

The Viking Age lasted from the late 700s to about 1100. Viking **warriors** looked for riches. Viking explorers looked for rich farmland. Viking settlers set up homes in new lands. The first map above shows the Vikings' world. Find the places where the Vikings lived.

The second map shows modern Scandinavia, the name given to the countries of Denmark, Norway, Sweden, and Iceland. Today, Scandinavia includes Finland, but the Finns long ago weren't Vikings. These lands have long, cold winters because they are so far north.

Norway and Sweden form a **peninsula**. This is a piece of land that is almost surrounded by water. Sweden has many lakes and forests. Much of Norway is mountainous. Norway has valleys and plains and many **fjords** (fyohrds) too. They are long, narrow inlets of the sea bordered by steep slopes.

Part of Denmark is also on a peninsula. The rest of Denmark is on islands. Iceland is an island in the Atlantic Ocean. Compare the two maps. Why do you think the Vikings were such great sailors?

The city of Bergen on the west coast of Norway

During the Viking Age, Viking ships were the best in the world. Using these fine ships, the Vikings sailed to many places. They traveled to the sunny Mediterranean Sea and icy Greenland. They also sailed across the Atlantic Ocean to North America.

LOOKING BACK

When the Vikings sailed, they used the sun and stars to help direct their course. They also used their knowledge of sea birds, fish, and wind and wave patterns to guide them at sea.

A Viking carving of a ship full of warriors

COMMUNITY LIFE

RULERS AND GOVERNMENT

Viking society **long ago** was divided into three classes: nobles, freemen, and slaves. Nobles were kings, chiefs, and other wealthy people. Freemen farmed or traded. Most Vikings were free.

The Vikings captured people during wars or raids. These people became slaves. Sometimes, slaves were freed as a reward for their good work. Others could buy their freedom.

A king or chief was the ruler of a community. But these rulers did not make all the decisions. In every Viking community, freemen and nobles belonged to an assembly called the *thing*. Members of the *thing* made laws.

Today, all Scandinavians are free. The countries are **democracies**, governments that are run by the people. Scandinavians who are at least 18 can vote for lawmakers.

An early Viking assembly in Iceland hears a divorce case in this painting.

A fisherman hangs his catch to dry.

WORK

In Scandinavia **long ago**, many Vikings were farmers. Good farmland lay in narrow strips along the coasts. Farmers raised pigs, cows, sheep, and chickens.

Farmers also grew grains, such as barley, rye, and oats. In the cold climate, they had to grow hardy vegetables, such as peas, beans, and cabbage. Other Vikings fished.

Some Viking metalworkers made necklaces and rings. Others made swords and spears. They also made simple tools, such as hammers and saws. Weavers, usually women, wove wool to make cloth. Carpenters built ships. Other Vikings were **merchants**. They bought, sold, and traded goods.

Viking men did not always stay at home. They sailed rivers and seas in search of gold, silver, and jewels. They took what they wanted by force. Anyone who tried to stand in their way was wounded or killed. They attacked towns and religious communities. Often these were left in ruins.

Today, some Scandinavians farm or fish. Norwegians continue to build ships. Scandinavian artists still make fine jewelry. Both Denmark and Sweden have skilled furniture builders. Many Swedes work in automobile factories. Many Scandinavians today work in education, banking, government, or health care.

A reproduction of a Viking house (left) and an ironing board made from whalebone (below)

HOMES

Most Vikings in Scandinavia **long ago** built their homes from wood. Roofs were made of wood shingles, **turf**, or straw. Thick mats of grass on the roof kept the house warm. The roof was green with grass in summer. It was white with snow in winter.

Imagine a single dark and smoky room. This was home for most Vikings. Some homes had one big room with a smaller room at either end. In winter, Vikings shared their homes with their animals. A door separated them. Think of the smell!

Vikings cooked over an open fireplace in the middle of the big room. Most of the smoke escaped through a hole in the roof. The fire heated and lit the room. Vikings also used candles and oil lamps for light.

Vikings decorated their homes with rugs and wall hangings. They built benches along the inside walls of their houses. They spread furs, blankets, and pillows on the benches at night.

Today, Scandinavians live in modern homes and apartments. Most live in cities.

Viking parents **long ago** usually chose the person each of their children would marry. Often, the best person was the one with the most property or goods.

Viking women had more rights than other women of that time. Viking women could own property and land. A wife shared her husband's wealth.

Men farmed and went to sea as warriors. Women made clothes, cooked, and did the housekeeping. Women ran the household when the men were away.

Viking children did not go to school. Instead, they learned skills from their parents. **Today**, all Scandinavian children must go to school for at least nine years, until they are age 16. Scandinavians are among the best-educated people in the world. Nearly everyone can read and write.

Students in a Swedish school

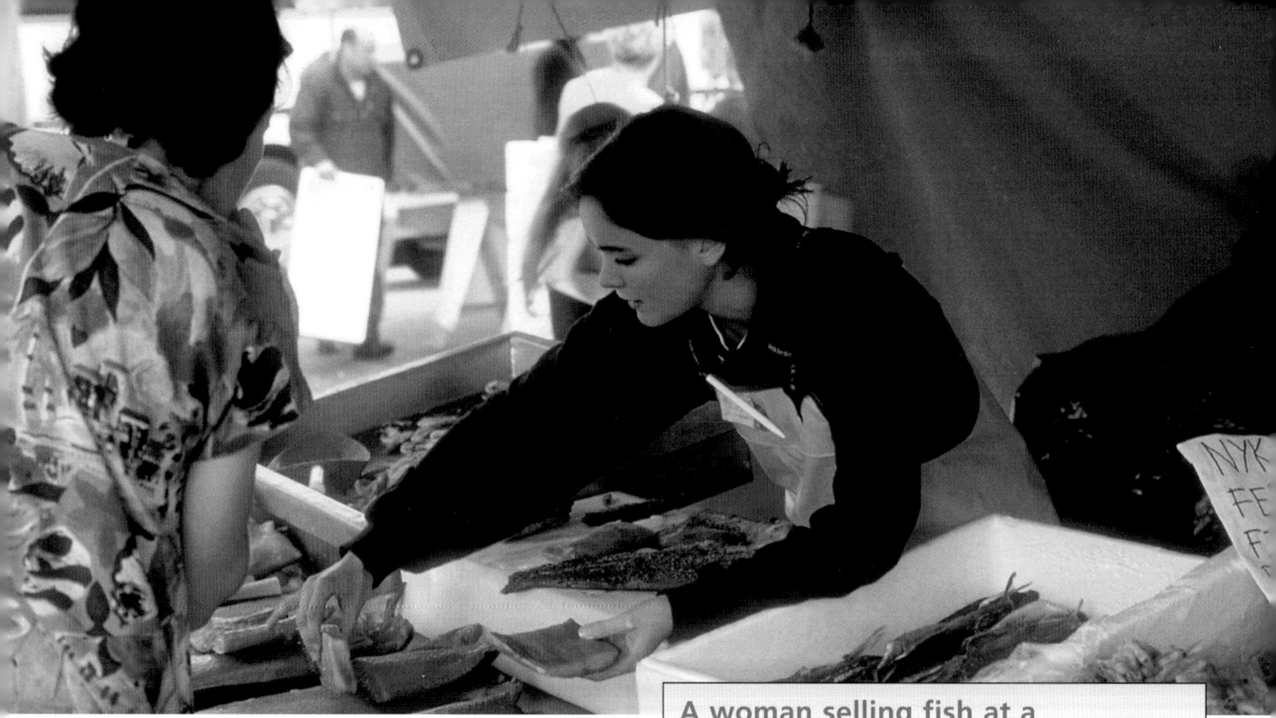

A woman selling fish at a Norwegian market

FOOD

In Scandinavia **long ago,** Vikings raised animals for meat. They hunted deer and seals. They ate fish, such as cod, trout, herring, and salmon.

Vikings dried or salted meat and fish. This made the food last through the winter. They also ate wild berries and apples.

Vikings ate eggs, drank milk, and made butter and cheese. They baked bread and made pancakes and porridge.

Today, Scandinavians eat many of the same kinds of foods that the Vikings ate. They eat other foods too. Open-faced sandwiches are popular. People start with one slice of bread. They put a topping such as shrimp, smoked herring, or cheese on it.

LOOKING BACK

Vikings ate two meals a day. They ate at about eight in the morning and again at about seven in the evening. People ate with their fingers and with knives and spoons. There were no forks.

CLOTHES

In Scandinavia **long ago**, Viking freemen wore woolen pants and a long shirt. Women wore long, loose-fitting dresses. Vikings also wore leather shoes. In winter, people wore capes, or cloaks, and fur hats to keep warm.

Nobles wore the same style of clothes as freemen did. Colorful embroidery sometimes decorated their clothes. Men and women wore beautiful pins to fasten their clothing.

Warriors wore leather caps or iron helmets to protect their heads in battle. Many warriors wore a leather **tunic** made from animal hide. Other warriors wore armor made of metal links called *chain mail*.

Today, Scandinavians wear the same kinds of clothes that people in most countries do. Many people wear jeans. Like the Vikings, some people wear fur hats in cold weather.

THEN & NOW

Long ago, most Europeans seldom took baths or changed their clothes. The Vikings took a bath about once a week. Some took a sauna. A sauna is a steam bath made by pouring water over hot stones. **Today,** people in many parts of the world enjoy taking a sauna.

A man wearing chain mail under a helmet

SHIPS, TRADE, AND EXPLORATION

SHIPS

Vikings in Scandinavia **long ago** were great boat builders. Their ships were strong and speedy. Vikings built their ships with wooden planks held together with metal pins.

Viking ships were light and easy to steer. They could travel in shallow water. They could move quickly down rivers and be pulled up on beaches. So, it was easy to catch people unaware.

On a windy day, a crew raised the sails on a ship. When there was no wind, a crew could row a ship. It took as many as 30 sailors to row some ships.

Unlike other ships built at that time, Viking ships could move forward or backward. So, Vikings did not have to waste time turning their boats around. They could attack quickly and make a fast escape.

A modern boat sails through a fjord in Norway.

Vikings built boats in different sizes. Longships were used for fighting wars. They were the fastest ships. Trading ships were shorter and wider, so they could carry more goods.

Today, just as in Viking times, people travel by boat on the fjords and rivers of Norway. Boats also move passengers and goods in Denmark and Sweden. Many people enjoy sailing their own boats in summer.

LOOKING BACK

Some wealthy Viking men and women were buried in ships. Many of their possessions, such as clothes, jewels, and household goods, were buried with them. Sometimes, pets and slaves were killed and buried with their owners. Vikings believed that the dead would then sail into the next world.

A modern crew sails a copy of a Viking longship.

A painting of Vikings sailing to Russia

TRADE AND EXPLORATION

The Vikings sailed far from their homes in Scandinavia **long ago**. They traded furs and **amber** for silver, silk, spices, and other goods. Amber is the hardened sap from ancient trees. It is used for making jewelry.

The Vikings sailed to coastal towns in the British Isles, Italy, and Spain. They sailed east to what is now Russia. They started trading centers in many eastern cities.

Tiny leaves and insects trapped in amber

Vikings wanted land as well as riches. Explorers from Norway sailed west to Iceland and settled there. Viking **descendants** live in Iceland today. Vikings also settled Greenland. They called the island Greenland, even though most of the year it is not green. They hoped the name would make people want to settle there.

Today, the peaceful Scandinavian countries trade with one another and with other countries. Denmark **exports** meat, fish, dairy products, furniture, ships, and machinery. Denmark **imports** chemicals, foods, and other goods.

Like Denmark, Norway imports food, chemicals, and machinery. Norway also has a big oil industry. Sweden's export goods include cars, paper, wood, and chemicals.

MEET LEIF ERIKSSON

Leif Eriksson was the son of a Viking explorer who went to Greenland. About A.D. 1000, Leif sailed to find land to the west of Greenland. According to Viking sagas, or stories, he found a place he called Vinland. Leif spent the winter there. Then he sailed back to Greenland. Archaeologists have found the remains of a Viking settlement in Newfoundland, Canada. They think this area may have been Vinland.

RELIGION AND RUNE STONES

A picture stone with letters called runes

In Scandinavia **long ago**, the Vikings believed in many different gods. Their gods had special powers, but they looked and behaved like people.

Odin (OH-dihn) was the most important Viking god. He was the god of battle, power, poetry, and wisdom. His many children were also gods and goddesses.

The Vikings believed in life after death. Some Vikings buried the dead with the things they would need in the next life. Other Vikings believed that the dead should be burned, together with the things they would need.

MEET THOR

Thor was Odin's oldest son. Viking **myths** describe Thor as a kind, honest, strong, and hungry god. In one myth, he ate an ox and eight salmon. Thor was also the Viking god of thunder and farming. He rode in a chariot pulled by goats. Vikings believed that thunder was the sound of Thor's chariot crossing the sky. They thought lightning was caused by Thor throwing his magic hammer. Thursday is named after Thor.

A stave church in Norway

Vikings sometimes carved stones to tell about a dead person's life. Some stones were carved with pictures. Others were carved with **runes**, characters from the Viking alphabet. The stones were put in places where many people would see them.

Today, most Scandinavians are Christians. They don't believe in the Viking gods. Much of the information we have about the Vikings' religious beliefs comes from sagas and poems. These sagas and poems were told for many generations. They were written down long after the Viking Age had ended.

LOOKING BACK

Through their raiding and trading, Vikings learned about Christian beliefs. Some Vikings married Christians. They took Christian beliefs back to Scandinavia. They built wooden churches called *stave churches* because their walls are made of planks of wood, or staves. Carved Viking dragons and Christian crosses decorate the roofs.

ENTERTAINMENT

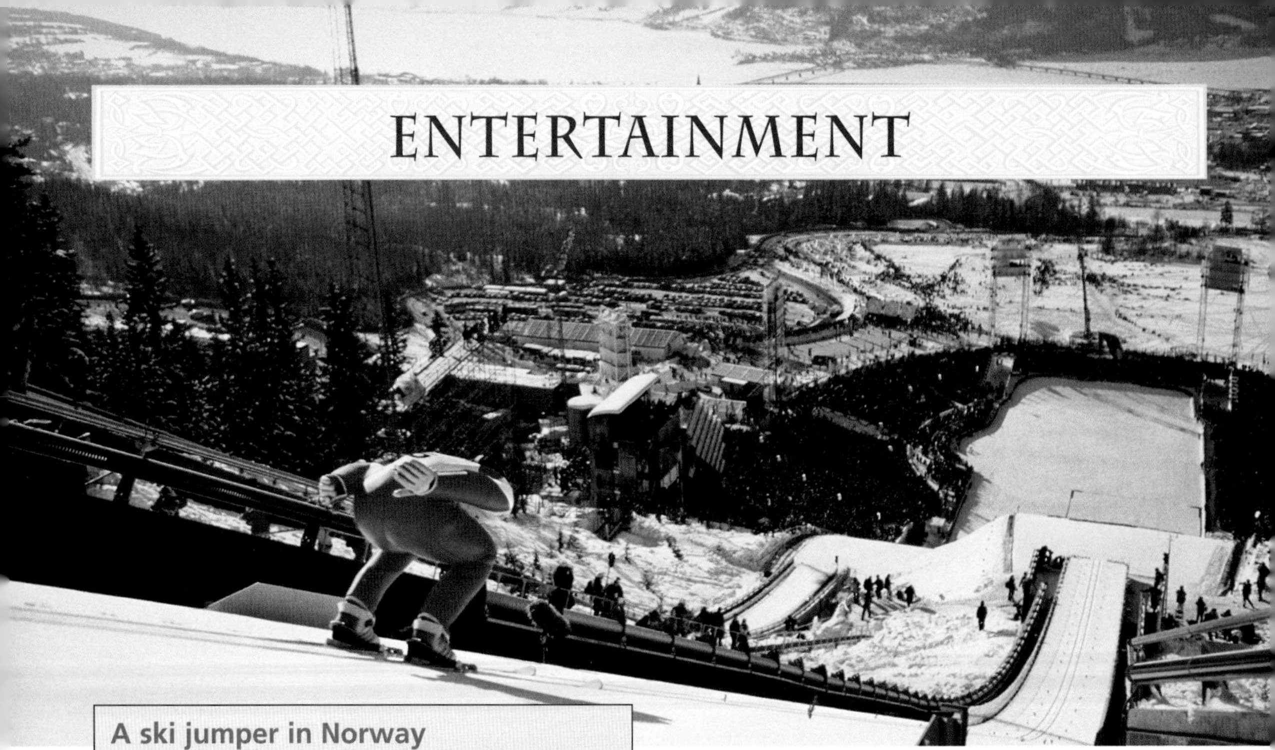

A ski jumper in Norway

Winters in Scandinavia are long. Viking children **long ago** spent winter evenings listening to poets, called *skalds*, tell of great adventures. Vikings loved to hear stories and poems about Viking gods and battles. These stories were passed on from one generation to the next.

Viking kings had their own skalds. A skald went with a king into battle. The poet would recite his poems to bring good luck to the king. Later, the skald would create poems to tell how brave the king was.

The ancient Vikings enjoyed such sports as rowing, swimming, and wrestling. In winter, they liked skiing and skating. They made skates from the long bones of horses, elk, or other animals. They tied the bones to their shoes. Chess and other board games were popular too.

Viking chess pieces made from walrus tusks

Today, Scandinavians enjoy outdoor sports just as the Vikings did. Books tell the same tales the skalds told long ago. Watching television and playing computer games are also popular pastimes.

Scandinavians also enjoy going to art and history museums. Visitors to Roskilde, Denmark, can see Viking ships at the Viking Ship Museum. In Copenhagen, they can go to an amusement park called Tivoli Gardens.

Many Scandinavians go to concerts, plays, and movies. And many of today's children enjoy the stories of Danish writer Hans Christian Andersen.

A statue of the Little Mermaid, a character from a Hans Christian Andersen fairy tale, in Copenhagen's harbor

People in traditional clothes enjoying a summer festival

CONTRIBUTIONS

The Vikings lived more than a thousand years ago. Yet, people today are still interested in their world.

Viking myths and poems have inspired modern writers, artists, and composers. Museum exhibits about Vikings attract crowds of people. Archaeologists continue to study runes and objects found in Viking burial grounds.

Modern sailboats in Norway

Today's world has other Viking influences. The Vikings were the first people to use a jury of 12 ordinary men to decide a law case. Vikings brought their democratic way of lawmaking and solving problems to countries they settled, such as Iceland.

Many of the words we use every day come from old Scandinavian languages. Some of these words are *cow*, *husband*, and *sky*. Also, there's a football team in Minnesota whose name comes from the subject of this book—the Vikings.

GLOSSARY

amber the sap from ancient trees that has hardened. It is used to make jewelry.

archaeologist a person who finds out about the past by digging up and studying old buildings and objects

democracy a government that is run by the people

descendant a person born of a certain family or group

export to send goods out of the country for sale or use in another

fjord a long, narrow bay of the sea bordered by steep cliffs

import to bring goods in from another country for sale or use

merchant a person who buys and sells for profit

myth a story, often one that tries to explain something in nature

peninsula a piece of land extending out into the water

rune a character in the alphabet used by the Vikings

saga a Viking story that tells of brave deeds

Scandinavia a region of northern Europe that includes Norway, Sweden, Denmark, Finland, and Iceland

tunic a long, loose-fitting shirt

turf a layer of soil that is covered with grass and other small plants

Vikings a people who lived in Scandinavia from the 700s to the 1100s

warrior a person who is experienced at fighting battles

A Viking brooch, or pin, shaped like a snake

INDEX

Andersen, Hans Christian 21

baths 4, 13

climate 6, 10
clothes 13, 21

education 11
entertainment 20–21
Eriksson, Leif 17
exploration 5, 6, 7, 16–17

family 11
farming 9
fishing 9
food 9, 12

geography 5, 6
government 8, 22

homes 10

jewelry 9, 16, 23
jury 22

myths 18, 22

Odin 18

religion 5, 15, 18–19
rulers 8
runestones 18–19, 22

sagas 17, 19, 23
saunas 13
ships and shipbuilding 4, 5, 7, 9, 14–15, 21
society 8
sports 20–21

Thor 18
trade 14, 16–17

Vinland 17

women 9, 11
work 9, 11

A rune stone showing a Viking god